John Alexander Joyce

Peculiar Poems

John Alexander Joyce

Peculiar Poems

ISBN/EAN: 9783744652261

Printed in Europe, USA, Canada, Australia, Japan

Cover: Foto ©Thomas Meinert / pixelio.de

More available books at **www.hansebooks.com**

Yours sincerely
John A. Joyce,

BY

COLONEL JOHN A. JOYCE

The ideal is the real !

———

Poets are all who feel great truths and tell them,
and the truth of truths is love !—*From Festus*

———

He talks of love and he dreams of fame,
And lauds his minstrel art ;
He has a kind of zig-zag brain
But yet—a straight line heart !—*Lamar*

NEW YORK

THOMAS R. KNOX & CO.

SUCCESSORS TO JAMES MILLER

813 BROADWAY

1885

TROW'S
PRINTING AND BOOKBINDING COMPANY,
NEW YORK.

Dedication

I DEDICATE THIS VOLUME TO MY DAUGHTER

FLORENCE,

WHOSE BEAMING BLUE EYES INDICATE A POETIC SOUL
AND WHOSE IMPULSIVE ACTION GIVES ASSURANCE OF FUTURE RENOWN.
THE LOVE OF A FATHER FOR HIS DAUGHTER IS THE RICHEST JEWEL IN THE
SANCTUARY OF AFFECTION.
I INVOKE THE SYMPATHY OF ALL PARENTS,
WHO WATCH WITH FEAR AND PRIDE THE IMAGE OF THEMSELVES CLIMBING
THE THORNY PATHS AND MOUNTAIN STEEPS OF LIFE,
AND WHILE WE MAY NOT KNEEL AT THE SAME ALTAR WE CAN WORSHIP
AT THE SHRINE OF A DAUGHTER'S LOVE.

PREFACE.

I HAVE no excuse to offer in sending this volume of poems out to the ocean of public opinion. They have been written for newspapers, magazines and persons at various times during the past twenty-five years. Many of them have gone the rounds of the press as "anonymous" waifs, and many of my rhythmic children are still travelling *incog*.

If the world takes half the pleasure in reading the poems that I felt in writing them, I shall be richly paid for their composition.

Truth and beauty are the bed-rock principles of poetry, and unless these two great elements conjoin in verse, there can be no poetry.

I do not claim for my lines the imperial flights of Homer, Shakspeare, or Edgar Allan Poe, but I do claim some of the simplicity, heart, and love found in Tasso, Goldsmith, Longfellow, and the Cary sisters.

Human nature has been the same since the world began, and he who can bring his bunch of roses to the fireside of simple love and trust, will see blushes of affection and feel warm responses of the heart.

There is not a poem in this book that has not a fact of my own experience as a basis, and while there are rollicking lines that might be cut out, I propose to leave them for the world that laughs, and for the "boys" and "girls" who appreciate fun and are not too good to acknowledge their humanity.

J. A. J.

CONTENTS.

8 CONTENTS.

CONTENTS. 9

PECULIAR POEMS.

THE STORY OF THE SAGE.

I MET a sage, decrepit, old and gray,
  While plodding through his last declining day,
And asked him, as he wandered down the vale,
To tell me of his life's eventful tale.
He leant upon his staff and paused awhile,
Then gazed across the sea to some fair isle
That met his fading vision through the gloom,
Where roses blossom in eternal bloom.
Fair youth, he said, my well-remembered years
Arise before me now through smiles and tears,
And take me back to love-lit, golden hours,
When life was young, amid sweet fragrant flowers;
My hopes were of the golden time to be,
Or like a full-rigged ship upon the sea—
Freighted with all the flashing hues of mind
That thrill the soul or deify mankind.
My boyhood pleasure was as bright as thine—
Came lightly as the foam on rosy wine ;

But like the foam it quickly passed away
And left me to another doubtful day.
I fondly thought that when my manhood came
I'd rush into the ranks and win a name
That ages yet unborn would emulate,
And grant me glory in both Church and State.
In blooming age I sought for power and place,
And won distinction in full many a race;
But just as sweet perfection came to view
The bowl was dashed and left me trials anew.
I sought the field of glory and of war,
My hope as bright as yonder evening star ;
And there I heard the shot and shrieking
    shell
That roared in terror, like a voice from hell.
Upon the ramparts high I waved my flag,
And struggled bravely up the mountain crag ;
But just as Victory o'er me threw her spell
I dropped the flag, faltered, wounded fell.
A broken soldier who has known defeat
Can fight and fall, but never can retreat,
And now you see me just the sport of Fate,
Its taunting voice still ringing out—too late.
In legislative halls with words ornate
I shone amid the thunders of debate,
And reaped some glory with a loud applause
For making many wholesome, honest laws.

I walked among the noble and the great
Who stood as pillars to the rising State ;
And while Dame Fortune promised every prize,
I only caught a glimpse of her bright eyes.
Yes, I have known a loving maid's embrace,
Whose soul shone brightly in her cheering face,
While laughing children clambered on my knee,
And blessed me with the glory of their glee.
Yet these have gone and left me weak and lone,
With nothing here that I can call my own,
Like yon bare pine that topples to decay,
And droops above where all its fellows lay ;
Or like an eagle on some mountain height,
With longing eyes, peers through the gathering
    night,
Awaiting one that never shall again
Soar with him grandly o'er the hill and plain.
Then I had friends who filled my banquet hall,
They drank my sparkling wine, both one and all ;
But when they saw and knew that I might fall,
They left me rudely with life's bitter gall !
But why repine for pleasure that is past,
Or sigh for earthly power that cannot last ;
While people praise us for their fame and joy
Erecting idols they will soon destroy ?
I wandered many years in foreign lands
From arctic regions to bright tropic sands,

Seeking for perfect pleasure on the way,
But never found it to the present day.
In beauty's eyes, from Persia to Peru,
I caught love glances as they darted through
The veil that cruel custom seeks to hide
What nature gave to show with honest pride.
In Florence and in Rome I looked aghast
At works of art that told me of the past,
Which peopled every crumbling tower and
　　pile　　　　　　　　　　　　　.
With royal spirits from some fairy isle.
The glowing canvas and the marble bust
Have rescued heroes from the thickening dust
That centuries of time accumulate
Upon the name of those who serve the State ;
But yet, the time will come when even the great
Are lost within the ruins of their State,
And every glorious fame that thrilled the past
Shall perish from the earth and die at last.
Ah ! here to-day you find me old and gray,
A wreck where once ambition held its sway ;
Where every romance in the soul of youth
Came lightly as the angel of the truth.
Now you are young, and like the noble pine,
But sure as fate, your steps must follow mine—
While you may hear and see what I have seen,
Your name be mentioned in immortal green ;

Yet still remember that no power or gold
Can purchase an exemption to grow old.
One hundred years have crowned my troubled way,
And here I crumble with my mother clay;
I'll take a last long look at yonder sun:
Farewell! farewell! My fleeting life is done!
He ceased, and sank into the gloom of night,
And left behind no ray of cheering light,
While all his conversation did but seem
The vestige of a vain and vanished dream!

GRANT'S MUSTERED OUT!

H ALF-MAST the flag, a heart brave and stout
Surrenders at last ; Grant's mustered out ;
Toll the bell slowly, moisten his sod,
Peace to his ashes, glory to God!

Battle and trial shall never again
Harrow the hero in sunshine or rain ;
He's gone to a land devoid of all doubt ;
All his service is over—Grant's mustered out.

His fame, like a light, shall shine through the
years,
Hallowed by memory and watered by tears—
Flags that he carried shall long flap and flout,
His record of glory we can't muster out!

Donelson, Shiloh, the Wilderness too,
Milestones immortal with deeds of the Blue :
And this is the man that never knew rout,
Till Fate told the world that, Grant's mustered out.

Nations unborn shall visit his tomb,
Reared by the people, and lasting as doom—
A Mecca where manhood may kneel without
doubt,
Where Truth everlasting is not mustered out!

KATIE AND I.

KATIE and I sat singing, singing
 As the moon went down ;
While bells were loudly ringing, ringing
 In the far off town.

Katie and I sat thinking, thinking
 Of the long ago ;
Sweet baby fingers lightly linking
 Memories under snow.

Katie and I soon sleeping, sleeping
 'Neath the silent sod ;
Our spirits fondly greeting, greeting
 Children, rest and God.

FAREWELL.

FAREWELL! farewell! My heart is sad and
  lonely,
While sailing o'er life's surging, stormy sea ;
My soul-lit thoughts are centred in thee only—
  The sweetest being in my memory.

Farewell! farewell! The secret of my longing,
  Cannot be told to those of common clay—
Yet, from the past your plighted vows come
    thronging,
  And thrill me with a love that could not stay.

Farewell! farewell! My bark is on the billow
  That hastens onward to a foreign shore ;
I fain would rest upon a fevered pillow,
  And still my weary soul forever more.

Farewell! farewell! Another hand shall lead thee,
  Another heart has won the prize I sought ;
Why, Oh! why could you rebuke, deceive me,
  And leave me lonely with this killing thought ?

Farewell! farewell! Thus are we doomed to sever,
  And break the tie that bound us to the past ;
Yet in my heart, forever and forever,
  I'll keep your sainted image to the last.

OCEAN MEMORIES.

(A SAN FRANCISCO SOUVENIR.)

YEARS have gone by since we met by the sea.
The kiss that you gave, love, lingers with
me ;
Thrills in my heart like an angelic tune,
Perfume distilled from the roses of June,
Silvery light from the face of the moon.

Lulled to repose by moan of the ocean,
Clasped in a thrill of blissful emotion,
Sunlight and starlight we catch but a gleam ;
The world is afloat : we live in a dream,
And things are not surely all that they seem.

Your secret and gem I still fondly keep
So close to my heart, awake or asleep ;
The world has no treasure dearer to me ;
Unpurchased, unsought, love without fee,
Was that soul-thrilling gift down by the sea.

Absent and lonely my soul flies to thee,
Back to the shore of that sweet summer sea—

A land where the vine and the orange doth bloom,
And silver and gold its mountains entomb—
A paradise planted, rich with perfume.

Sadly I sigh for your loving embrace ;
Fancy awakens the light of your face ;
Out through the mists of yon echoless shore
Angels are calling my lost, loved Lacore,
Sighing I pine for your love evermore !

THE RAIN.

THE rain, the rain, the beautiful rain,
Descends on the grass and the golden grain;
Refreshing the leaves and the fading flowers,
Singing a song to the fleeting hours.

The murmuring rain, the gentle shower
Drips through the trees in the woodland bower,
Falls on the roof and sinks to the sea,
Where it waters the shores of memory.

Well I remember the days of old,
The cottage porch, and the love she told,
The rain that danced on the trailing vine,
And the beautiful hand that lay in mine.

The snow and the rain of long, long years
Have chilled my heart with the hopes and fears
That filled my soul in the long ago,
Before I had learned the weight of woe.

Her little mound in the churchyard near
I deck with a flower, spray and tear,
Mingle my sighs with the sounding rain,
And wish for that soft white hand again.

A few more days of pleasure and pain
And I shall sleep 'neath the falling rain,
And all the living above the sod
Must leave their trials and go to God.

It matters little to you or to me
Whether we die on the land or the sea ;
The sun will shine and the rain will fall
And a generous grave will hide us all.

THE CRICKET.

L ITTLE cricket, standing picket
   Near the blazing hearth,
Chirping lightly, blithe and brightly,
   Whence thy early birth?

Sing away my little cricket,
   Time is on the wing—
Live the hours in warm bowers
   Chirping in the spring.

Who can tell the nameless longing
   In thy sable crest?
Who can tell the thoughts now thronging
   In the cricket's breast?

LOVE.

CLASP me to your warm embrace ;
    Take me to your loving heart ;
Let me feel your velvet face
    Breast to breast, and heart to heart,
    Nevermore to pine or part.

In your eyes my heaven is shining—
    Golden sunlight is your hair ;
All my clouds have silver lining
    While your spirit hovers there,
    And I see you everywhere.

As the river to the ocean,
    And the brooklet to the sea,
So my soul throbs with emotion,
    All its currents turn to thee,
    Faithful to eternity.

Thrill me with your passion kisses ;
    Fill me with a nameless joy ;
Earth has no such cherished blisses,
    Pleasure that we can't destroy,
    Virgin gold without alloy !

TOLL THE BELL.

TOLL the bell slowly, meekly, and lowly,
    There comes an inanimate clod,
Sleeping forever beyond the dark river
    A mortal has gone to his God.

Toll the bell faintly ; echoes so saintly
    Are sounding o'er river and lea,
Telling the living all need forgiving
    Before God and eternity.

Toll the bell lightly, daily and nightly
    A spirit is watching for thee,
One that has loved us, one that has proved us,
    Some fond soul who loved you and me.

Toll the bell sadly, heart-broken, madly
    We kiss the cold lips of the dead,
With hope, love, and tears, run back o'er the years
    To pluck out some cruel word said.

LINDALOU.

(DEDICATED TO HON. S. S. COX, U. S. MINISTER TO
TURKEY.)

I DRINK to the light of the harem,
As lithe as a classical faun,
A soft scintillation of pleasure,
A beautiful creature of dawn,
And frail as the dew on the lawn.

I sing to the light of the harem,
As she glides through the gilded saloon,
And floats like a sylph o'er a zephyr,
Who leaves me in sorrow too soon
When passion has reached its high noon !

I sigh for the light of the harem,
A sunbeam of magical hue,
A beauty, the rarest and fairest,
The pride of the Sultan—Boohoo,
My royal coquette, Lindalou.

I live in the light of the harem,
And bask 'neath those beautiful eyes,
Recline on rich Ottoman velvets
To gaze on the Bosphorus skies,
Lindalou and her sweet paradise.

BY THE SEA.

I AM standing by the sea,
   And I listen to the roar
Of the mighty ocean,
   As it breaks against the shore.

I think of Now and Then,
   And long for evermore
To taste of living wine
   On God's eternal shore.

I see the breaker coming,
   With a petrel on its crest ;
I plunge into the billow,
   Wildly crying, " Here is rest ! "

MAZY.

SHE sleeps on the hill near the crumbling
mill—
And my mind is nearly crazy
When I note the hours and faded flowers
Gone with the sun and the daisy.

Through the orchard wild, as a loving child,
She sported long in the clover ;
And the blossoms free from the apple-tree,
She heaped on her pet dog, Rover.

The bees she chased, in her laughing haste,
In the fields and nooks, so sunny ;
With roses red she decked her head—
And life was sweet as honey.

A few more years—a few more tears—
Will waft me away to Mazy ;
And I shall sleep where willows weep
By her side, 'neath the blooming daisy.

FLOWERS OF HOPE.

(DEDICATED TO M. J. MURPHY.)

THE sweetest flowers of golden hours
    Must fade and pass away;
But love or truth, of age or youth,
    Shall never know decay.

The hills are gray. Old Time wont stay,
    But keeps upon the wing;
Its flight of years bring smiles and tears
    To peasant, prince, and king.

Dear friends, depart; and leave the heart—
    A ruin old and lone—
With nothing here, from year to year,
    Which it can call its own.

Yet, o'er the gloom beyond the tomb,
    Where Hope can only see,
There is a rest among the blessed,
    And joy for you and me.

DECORATION POEM.

(SOLDIERS' HOME, WASHINGTON, D. C., MAY 30, 1885.)

WE celebrate and dedicate
  This day of blooming flowers
To those who fell for yonder flag,
  That starry flag of ours—
  Defying human powers.

Where'er we roam, this Soldiers' Home
  Can never be forgot,
While airs shall blow from Mexico
  To cheer our happy lot
  And sing of General Scott.

From sun to sun, while ages run,
  We'll sound in song and story
The record of these noble men
  Adown the aisles of glory,
  Who fought on fields so gory.

I hear again, o'er hill and plain,
  The cry and shot of battle—
The neighing steed, our wounded bleed,
  The roaring, tearing metal
  Where cannons loudly rattle.

These mounds shall be, to all the free,
  A shrine for loyal greeting,
Where we may kneel, in woe or weal,
  While happy hours are fleeting,
  At every May-time meeting.

The wild long-roll that thrill'd the soul
  No more for these resounding ;
But calm and still they top this hill,
  Where balmy airs are bounding,
  And life is not confounding.

And memory clings where love still sings
  Among these sacred bowers,
The livelong day in sunny May,
  With all its golden hours,
  And cool, refreshing showers.

No autumn blow, nor frost, nor snow,
  Can chill the love we cherished
For men so true, who wore the blue,
  In life their country nourished,
  And for that flag they perished.

Their loyal dust shall be a trust
  To this devoted nation,
That by their blood, on field and flood,
  Secured a new salvation,
  And gained great approbation.

No slave to-day pollutes our way
   From ocean unto ocean,
But great and free, on land and sea,
   Our flag floats with devotion—
   Sweet liberty its portion.

And o'er these graves it proudly waves
   Where roses blush in billows,
And forest leaves break ranks to grieve
   Above their soldier pillows,
   Around yon weeping willows.

At Sumter hot, where shell and shot
   Tore ramparts from their mooring,
These fought and fell in that red hell—
   A desperate alluring
   For country still enduring.

At Shiloh, too, these boys in blue
   Died for a splendid reason—
That faith and trust forever must,
   In every State and season,
   Crush out the hosts of treason.

In serried lines, mid oaks and pines,
   I see their bayonets flashing ;
These phantom hosts and sainted ghosts
   For Union still are dashing—
   A rude rebellion smashing.

Die for a plan, the rights of man,
   Our country, one in many,
Where all are blessed, and he is best
   That can't be false or canny,
   And will not stoop to any.

Let valor yield its sword and shield
   To patriots and freemen,
And honor bright both day and night
   Crown soldier and crown seamen,
   And scatter every demon.

And now so true, " the boys in blue "
   May group in one grand rally,
And strew with love to those above
   The flowers from hill and valley
   Along Dame Nature's alley.

Then as a band we'll firmly stand,
   Defying all creation ;
Round Northern pine the Southern vine
   May bloom in every station—
   A fragrant, sweet oblation.

Long may we live to smile and give,
   And feel no separation ;
But from this sod we'll look to God,
   And join in decoration—
   One grand, United Nation !

2*

WAITING.

HOW well I remember, darling,
   In the beautiful long ago,
When we pledged our love with kisses
   Down by the brooklet's flow,
   Where the shadows come and go.

Now, I am broken-hearted ;
   The light of my soul hath fled :
A weary pilgrim waiting
   To join the ranks of the dead,
   And lay down my weary head.

Alone in the moonlight watching,
   At her grave I lay me low,
While the winds are blowing by me
   And my darling under the snow,
   Buried forever, joy with woe.

FORGETTING.

THE friends that I loved in December
   And cherished so fondly in May,
Have long since forgot to remember,
   And vanished like dewdrops away.

In sunshine and power I was toasted
   And feasted by courtiers so kind ;
And, Oh ! how the parasites boasted
   Of the wonderful traits of my mind.

But when the dark hour of my trouble
   Arose like a storm in the sky,
The vipers began to play double,
   And forgot the bright glance of my eye !

GOD IS NEAR.

GOD is near upon the ocean,
    God is near upon the land;
He is All, both rest and motion—
    We are only grains of sand,
Little mites upon life's billow,
    May, flies buzzing out the hour,
Dreams upon a fevered pillow—
    Dewdrops on a withered flower;
Only waiting for to-morrow—
    That has never come to man,   .
Here we live in joy and sorrow,
    Chasing phantoms as we can,
Chasing pleasure, chasing greatness,
    Over tangled walks and waves;
But we learn the bitter lateness
    Just before we find our graves.
Hope is nigh with fairy fingers,
    Tracing sunbeams on the way;
Magic memory ever lingers,
    Busy with the bygone day.
Life and death are but the portals
    To a realm of endless rest;
God is working through his mortals;
    All in some way shall be blessed!

LOVE AND LAUGHTER.

(DEDICATED TO GEORGE D. PRENTICE, 1863.)

L AUGH, and the word laughs with you ;
   Weep, and you weep alone ;
This grand old earth must borrow its mirth,
   It has troubles enough of its own.
Sing, and the hills will answer ;
   Sigh, it is lost on the air ;
The echoes bound to a joyful sound
   But shrink from voicing care.

Be glad, and your friends are many ;
   Be sad, and you lose them all ;
There are none to decline your nectared wine,
   But alone you must drink life's gall.
There is room in the halls of pleasure
   For a long and a lordly train,
But one by one we must all file on
   Through the narrow aisles of pain.

Feast, and your halls are crowded ;
   Fast, and the world goes by ;

Succeed and give, 'twill help you live ;
  But no one can help you die.
Rejoice, and men will seek you ;
  Grieve, and they turn and go—
They want full measure of all your pleasure,
  But they do not want your woe!

THE SUNBEAM.

A BEAUTIFUL beam came into my cell,
  Fresh from the eye of Jehovah, to tell
That bolts and bars cannot keep out the light
Of truth, and justice, of mercy and right ;
It checkered the flags through the iron door,
And danced in the shadows that kissed the floor,
And loitered about in a friendly way,
Until beckoned back at the close of day ;
When out of the window, it flew on high
And hastened back to its home in the sky.
I followed the beautiful beam to rest,
To a sea of light in the golden west ;
It dropped to sleep on the dark blue sea
And left me the sweetest memory.
I turned to my soul for calm relief,
Balm to my wound, a check to my grief—
When visions of glory shone from above
Where the light is God, and God is love !

DREAMING.

DREAMING, dreaming, only seeming
    That I loved you long ago ;
Weeping, weeping, fondly keeping
    Secrets from both friend and foe.

Thinking, thinking, lightly linking
    All the hopes that filled the past ;
Peering, fearing, gently nearing
    To our promised joys at last.

MY BABY'S EYES.

(TO FLORENCE.)

MY baby's eyes in melting blue
Are beaming bright as morning dew,
And from the sky light take a hue,
Or like the star light bright and true.

My baby's eyes in liquid roll
Enhance my world from pole to pole,
And love sits smiling in that goal
Forever speaking to my soul.

My baby's eyes in other years
May fill with many scalding tears,
And yet through cruel taunts and jeers
A mother's love will banish fears.

My baby's eyes in blight or bloom,
Those glorious orbs in grief or gloom,
Shall be to me in death or doom,
The dearest diamonds to the tomb.

YOSEMITE.

YOSEMITE! grand and wonderful in thy
    lone beauty!
Valley of sweet enchantment.
In twilight hours my soul commingles with rock
    and waterfall.
To the front Cloud's Rest towers in the evening
    gold.
Like the ghost of vanished years its snowy crest
    rises o'er the gorge.
As a racehorse in his course runs the brawling
    Merced.
Rocky fragments from surrounding crags choke
    its peaceful flow.
The voices of Bridal Veil, Vernal and Nevada
    Falls speak to the echoes.
Centuries of sound answer.
The wail of the waters, unceasing, mourns lost
    races.
El Capitan,
Cathedral Spire and Liberty Cap rear their craggy
    crests into the upper blue.
Time's ceaseless chisel has left its deep traces on
    the mountain brow.

Rains, winds and suns, have deepened the wrinkles
on thy face, and furrowed thy rocky ribs.
Bald brow, stony heart and granite feet, defy the
wearing war of ages.
Earthquake pains and volcanic fires sent thee
forth.
The moulten, blazing columns sought the stars,
laughed in pride,
Shook their fiery locks, fixed themselves in space,
making the valley that lies between.
Sheltered from sunshine and storms:
Oaks and pines tremble as thy verdant locks,
And whispering vines and shrubs entwine thy
brow.
Thy snow-capped peaks are decked with blood-
red snow flowers—
Blooming in the home of eternal winter,
More beautiful than the royal jewels that crowned
the Egyptian Queen.
A lovely lake mirrors thy form, reflecting all that
looks on its crystal surface.
In moonlit hours go to its banks, feel the cool
winds on thy cheek,
And list to the murmuring manzaneta coquetting
with its sister leaves.
A million multiplied stars sparkle in the bosom
of the lake,

Variegated as a field of diamonds.
Pilgrims from all lands shall visit thy shade
through the crowding ages.
Memory will stamp thy features on the heart,
And blend the romance of the valley with the
last sigh of the traveller.
The red hunter has been swept away by the pale
race.
The crowding tramp of ages will roll over us in
turn,
Leaving no memorial to show where we rose or
fell.
Thou, Yosemite, shall stand a master monument,
Defying the gnawing tooth of Time, grand, and
eternal!

SECRET LOVE.

(DEDICATED TO MISS E. R. G.)

YOU have lived in my heart year after year,
And the secret I never have told ;
I think of you now with joy and with fear,
But you're haughty, and heartless, and cold.

My nature is honest, loving and true,
Yet I sigh in the depths of my soul
For one word of love that will bring me to you,
My ideal, my fate, and my goal.

My love may be crushed with your coldness,
And my heart may be withered by care,
But I never can tell you with boldness,
Of the love that I secretly bear.

I see you in crowds shining brightly,
And my soul swells with pride at your fame ;
Every word in your praise, though so slightly,
Thrills my heart at the sound of your name.

And you never will know of my weeping,
Nor the love that I coyly enshrine ;
For daily and nightly I'm keeping
Precious thoughts that can only be mine.

QUESTION AND ANSWER.

QUESTION.

WILL you love me, darling Katie,
    When my steps are weak and slow?
Will you love me ever truly,
    Through the vale of joy and woe?

Will you love me when the world
    Frowns, and looks with scorning eye?
Will you love me till the moment
    When I heave the parting sigh?

Will you love me when I'm gone,
    As you love me now while here?
Will your heartbeats ever linger
    On my name throughout the year?

Will you love me in the springtime?
    Will you love me in the fall?
Can I count on you in winter
    When the snow hangs over all?

ANSWER.

I shall love you in misfortune,
  With all my heart and soul ;
I shall never cease to love thee
  While the stars around me roll.

Then, darling, never doubt me
  In the turns of time so strange,
My star of love shall never set,
  My heart shall never change.

But life and love I'll give thee—
  Thy bride in truth was cast ;
My heart and soul, fondly thine—
  Dear, darling, to the last.

Yes, Willie, I shall love thee
  When your locks are growing gray ;
I shall love you in December
  With the love I gave in May!

THE FATHERLAND.

(TO MEIN FRAU.)

I WILL drink to my own Fatherland,
  To the crags and the vales of the Rhine,
Where the rugged old castles still stand,
  And the hills blush with grape and with wine.

'Tis there, in the morning of childhood,
  I wandered as free as a fawn ;
And echoes I heard in the wildwood
  Were pure as the dew and the dawn.

The landscape and Black Forest mountain
  Are pictured in memory by me,
And every Rhine rock and fair fountain
  Sings the song of the fatal Lorelei !

THE OLD HOMESTEAD.

I GAZE on my old ruined homestead to-day
Through the tears of a wild, vanished youth ;
I see the broad porches gone down to decay
Where my mother instilled every truth.

The chimney has crumbled away in the blast,
And the rafters have all tumbled down ;
The hearthstone brings back all the joys of the
past
As the clouds in the west darkly frown.

The spring at the foot of the hill has gone dry,
And the apple and plum trees have gone ;
I stand in the gloom as the winds deeply sigh—
See the ghosts of my friends one by one.

Here, my mother and father sleep side by side
In a nook on the top of the hill ;
Where my heart was as light as the foam on the
tide
When I sauntered about the old mill

That stood on the banks of the creek, down the
     lane,
Where it rumbled its musical flow;
But alas ! I shall never play there again
     As I played in the sweet long ago.

The woodpecker drums o'er my head on the oak
     And the gray squirrel chatters his tune,
But where are the schoolmates whose sport and
     whose joke
Thrilled my heart in the play-spell at noon.

Some are "gone o'er the ranges" to sleep in the
     vale ;
Like myself, some have wandered afar—
Blown about like a leaf in a withering gale
     Or attuned like a broken guitar.

By the last ray of sunset I sadly behold
     The old ruined home of my youth,
Where the jessamine clambered in colors of gold,
     And the voices I heard spoke the truth.

Farewell to the scenes and the friends that I
     knew
In the morning of life, bright and fair—
My heart shall forever commingle with you
     And my spirit shall always be there !

TRAPPINGS OF CLAY.

THESE trappings of clay shall moulder away
   And leave not a vestige behind ;
But Truth in its bloom shall rise o'er the tomb
   To glorify God-given mind.

A very few years commingled with fears
   Are all that each mortal can claim,
With some little joy—a bauble or toy—
   One blast from the trumpet of Fame.

And then we are naught, as if never brought
   To dance out our poor little day
In a world of care, bleak, barren and bare—
   So lonesome, and passing away.

But while we are here let's join in the cheer,
   And laugh with a merry good will,
Throw care to the wind, and ever be kind
   To those who are climbing the hill

That points to a land, rich, blooming and grand
   Where virtue shall ever be blessed,
And all who are true, whether many or few,
   Shall cease from their labors and rest.

SIR MOSES MONTEFIORE.

(DEDICATED TO HON. SIMON WOLF, 1884.)

A HUNDRED years of glorious life
Have crowned our royal hero,
The best of all in Hebrew strife—
Sir Moses Montefiore.

A hundred years of love and truth
Have blessed his deep devotion
For those oppressed in age or youth,
Enchained on land or ocean.

A hundred years of richest dower
Have made him great in beauty,
Like David in his Psalms of power—
Like Solomon in duty.

A million years cannot efface
The record of the good,
Nor blot from earth the Jewish race—
Our ancient brotherhood.

Across the seas we grasp a hand
  That reaches down the ages ;
Still pointing to the promised land
  With all its golden pages.

A life of love and deeds sublime
  Shall live in song and story,
And stand the test of tide and time
  Adown the aisles of glory.

For Montefiore and his line
  We'll make the welkin ring,
And drink his health in living wine—
  Love's monarch, prince and king.

THE LEAVES ARE FALLING.

THE leaves are falling ; I hear you calling
· From out the years that slumber in the past,
Asleep or waking, my heart is breaking
    For one sweet love that thrills it to the last.

The leaves are sailing, and I'm bewailing
    The lost affections of my vanished youth,
When friends were dearer, and hearts were nearer,
    And life was in the heaven of their truth.

The leaves are flying, the winds are sighing,
    And Nature with her garb of green and gray
Makes many changes o'er hill and ranges—
    A bride of beauty in her autumn day.

Along the hours, in golden showers
    The leaves are falling o'er hill and dale ;
Their ranks are broken—a voiceless token
    That we shall follow down the fading vale
    And perish like the leaves blown by the gale.

But still while thinking, my soul is linking
    Unto celestial lands beyond this sod,
Where peace and pleasure beyond all measure
    Shall crown us 'neath the chast'ning golden rod,
    Amid the realms of glory and of God.

I WANT.

I WANT to cry and scratch when first I see,
  I want a constant care through infancy,
I want a rattle and a rubber ring,
I want my "mamma dear" to play and sing;
I want a flying kite and spinning top,
I want some candy and some ginger pop.
I want to go to school and learn to read,
I want to go to church and hear the creed.
I want a sweetheart who is kind and true,
I want some darling always bright to view.
I want a cottage by the sounding sea,
I want a wife that loves no one but me.
I want great honors in the march of mind,
I want the wealth that Crœsus left behind.
I want a mansion near some rustic lake,
I want a love as light as the snowflake.
I want fine horses, hounds, and servants rare,
I want a life entirely free from care.
I want the years to glide as fast as hours,
I want the moments perfumed by the flowers.
I want to sail upon the ocean tide,
I want to wander o'er the world wide.

I want my youth to ripen into age,
I want the sense that settles in the sage.
I want more gold and gems to grace my life,
I want bright children and a winsome wife.
I want the music of the light guitar,
I want rare books, collected near and far.
I want to bask 'neath orange-trees and limes,
I want the song of birds from tropic climes.
I want to scale the mountains to the sun,
I want companions when the day is done.
I want the sparkling wine so richly stored,
I want it always on my festive board.
I want the laughter and the beaming eye,
I want fair beauties who can sing and sigh.
I want a couch of purple and of lace,
I want a fairy form, ever face to face.
I want the moonbeams through my lattice calm,
I want the murmur of love's healing balm.
I want the winds to lull me to repose,
I want to taste the dewdrop on the rose.
I want a mind that's ever pure and just,
I want a heart that's filled with loving trust.
I want a soul that soars beyond the earth,
I want to know the region of its birth.
I want to act a noble part with man,
I want to always do the best I can.
I want to be content and live at ease,

I want, in fact, to do just what I please.
I want to rest in an immortal bloom,
I want sweet flowers to grow upon my tomb.
I want, and wish, and yet I do deplore,
I still shall want until I am no more.

3*

LONG LIVE THE UNION.

(TO THE PRESIDENT.)

LONG live the Union of States and of hearts—
A nation of love in all of its parts,
From Northland, Southland, East, and great West
E PLURIBUS *Unum*—grandest and best.

Long live the nation, its laws, and its chief,
May it never know trouble, rupture, or grief;
Long live our country, happy and free
From the lakes to the gulf, on to the sea.

Long live Columbia, the hope of the world;
Its banner of glory shall never be furled;
Its stripes and its stars an emblem shall be
Of brothers that rule in the land of the free.

Long live the voice of the people who reign,
Sounding forever o'er hilltop and plain—
Long live our Chief and pure be his praise,
Green be his laurels and bright be his days.

THERE'S NO POCKET IN A SIIROUD!

(ON THE DEATH OF A MILLIONAIRE.)

YOU must leave your many millions
    And the gay and festive crowd ;
Though you roll in royal billions,
    There's no pocket in a shroud.

Whether pauper, prince or peasant ;
    Whether rich or poor or proud—
Remember that there isn't
    Any pocket in a shroud.

You'll have all this world of glory
    With a record long and loud,
And a name in song and story,
    But no pocket in your shroud.

So be gen'rous with your riches,
    Neither vain, nor cold, nor proud,
And you'll gain the golden niches
    In a clime without a cloud !

WHEN I AM GONE.

(TO A DEAR FRIEND.)

WHEN I am gone from the heartless,
    And vanish from those who pursue,
The world may not hold me guiltless,
    Though it could not convict me with you.

Although the rude world rebuked me,
    And howled like a hound on my track,
Your love shone a glory around me—
    Smiled in beauty and beckoned me back.

When I am lost in the ocean
    That breaks on eternity's shore,
My spirit will smile in devotion,
    And soar with your love evermore.

THE HEART I LOVED.

(TO S. H.)

THE heart I loved has gone forever ;
The world has no more charm for me ;
My life is like a shallow river
That ripples lonely to the sea.

The heart I loved rests 'neath yon willow
That bends in beauty by the stream ;
Oh ! how I long to share her pillow,
And sink into some magic dream.

The flowers are blighted, and I'm benighted,
No sun for me shall shine again ;
The love I cherished has rudely perished
And left me like a desert plain.

A LONG LIGHTED VISTA.

I LOOK down a long lighted vista
    Where sunshine and shadows creep through,
And memory brings back the loved ones
    That pass in procession in view—
    The dear, honest friends that I knew.

I peer through that long lighted vista
    Where briers and flowers abound,
Were virtue and sin ever battle
    And pleasure can never be found,
    While sorrow pursues like a hound.

You ask for the place of this vista,
    Inquire from the pole to the pole,
The starlight and sunlight will answer—
    In the throb and the sigh of the soul
    Is the vista that leads to the Whole.

UNKNOWN.

I GAZED on the babe at its mother's breast,
  And asked for the secret of life and rest ;
It turned with a smile that was sad and lone,
And murmured in dreaming, "Unknown," "un-
  known."

I challenged the youth so bold and so brave,
To tell me the tale of the lonely grave ;
But he sung of pleasure in musical tone,
And his echoing voice replied " Unknown," " un-
  known."

Then I questioned the gray-haired man of years,
Whose face was furrowed with thoughts and tears ;
And he paused in his race to simply groan,
The soul-chilling words : " Unknown," " un-
  known."

I asked the lover, the poet and sage—
In every clime and in every age—
To tell me the truth, and candidly own
If after life it is all unknown.

I soared like the lark to the boundless sky,
Sighed in my soul for the how and the why ;
The angels were singing and just had flown ;
I heard but the echo, " Unknown," "unknown."

I read in the hills and saw in the rocks
A lesson that told of the earthquake shocks ;
I gazed at the stars from a mountain cone,
But they only answered—"Unknown, "unknown."

Thus am I tortured by fear and by doubts,
In tracing the way where so many routes
Are ever in view, and quickly are flown,
And all that I know is—"Unknown," "unknown."

At last I determined to surely find
All hope and all bliss in my mystic mind ;
But just as sweet peace came to soothe me alone,
The wild witch of doubt shrieked : " Unknown,"
"unknown."

The sun and the moon, the winds and the wave,
May perish in time and sink to the grave ;
The temples of earth shall fall, stone by stone,
And mortals still wail out—"Unknown," "unknown."

The millions of earth that battle to-day,
Are but a handful to those passed away ;
The future is countless—men from each zone
Shall flourish and die in the far-off unknown.

We come like the dewdrops and go like the mist,
As frail as a leaf by autumn winds kissed ;
Fading away like the roses of June—
Wishing and waiting to meet the unknown.

Nature, Oh! Nature, thy God I adore ;
There's light in thy realm, I ask for no more ;
From the seed to the fruit all things are grown,
Yet, while we know this, the cause is unknown.

When matter and mind are perished and lost,
And all that we see into chaos is tossed,
From nothing to nothing we pass out alone,
Like a flash or an echo—" Unknown," "un-
  known!"

WYOMING VALLEY.

FROM Prospect Rock I see afar
      Wyoming Valley, green and free,
Still sparkling like the morning star
   For labor and for liberty.

The Susquehanna rolls along
   In rippling beauty through the hills,
Resounding with a forest song
   And laughing, brawling, shining rills.

The hum of labor fills the air,
   The panting engine sweeps around
The upland slopes, and everywhere
   We wander o'er historic ground.

Yon island blooms within a vale
   Where crystal waters kiss the flowers,
And every sound that fills the gale
   Responds unto the golden hours.

Round, rolling ridges bold and high,
   The fragrant flowers of blooming may
Exhale their perfume to the sky
   And give to all a perfect day.

Where sun and stream and brook and hill
Commingle to entrance the scene,
And heart and soul with rapture fill
The life and love that lie between.

WILKESBARRE, PA., May, 1885.

WEDDING BELLS.

(KATIE'S TRIBUTE, MAY 13, 1879.)

RING out glad bells, ring out, I say!
This is the Golden Wedding Day;
Ring happy chimes to bring those near
Who love the homestead fond and dear.

Ring loud! ring strong! to bring the throng
Of all who to this home belong;
Bring here the happy and the sad,
For each will make these fond hearts glad.

Ring! ring! I say, that far away
Loved ones will hear what 'tis you say;
Ring once again to guide them here,
To smile upon this golden cheer.

Ring fifty strokes in golden tone!
For work of fifty years well done.
Ring fifty strokes! Each stroke attest,
Father, mother, each were best.

Ring for the past, the future too,
To pledges we this day renew;
Ring for our father, mother dear,
We pledge them with affection's tear.

THE BRIDGE.

(A PARODY.)

I STOOD on the bridge at midnight,
  As the planks were rotting away,
And a light shone o'er the city
  As the toll-bridge went to decay.

How often, oh! how often,
  In the days that had gone by,
I stopped at the bridge in daylight
  And paid my toll with a sigh.

For my heart was hot and restless,
  And my life was full of gall
At this crumbling relic of blackmail
  That must sink to a speedy fall.

Yet whenever I cross the river
  On this bridge with mouldering piers,
The odor of slavery stuns me
  And the darkness of vanished years!

MY LOVE.

MY love, my love comes over the sea ;
    He is thinking of nothing but love and me ;
The winds blow high and the storm-clouds sweep,
But my love still comes o'er the rolling deep.

My love, my love is nearing the shore—
My lonely waiting will soon be o'er,
And my loving arms so fond and free
Shall clasp him again from the stormy sea.

A sail's in sight, but the storm-winds roar,
The waves lash loud on this rocky shore—
And the ship that bears my love to me
Is swallowed up by the heartless sea!

DON'T GAMBLE IN STOCKS.

DON'T gamble in stocks—have tried it myself,
On many a bright rosy morn ;
Do what you may, you'll be put on the shelf—
"Come out, the small end of the horn."

I tackled K. T., and purchased Eric,
The morning I first got to "town ;"
But now I can see my fond prophecy—
The one to go up went right down.

I then "struck" Lake Shore and old Baltimore,
That was rated fine as pure gold ;
With "calls" by the score, and margins for more,
I found in the end I was sold.

I then tried W. U., and sound C. B. Q.,
Sold "short," and went "long" on O. T. ;
Had "puts" on U. P., and "calls" on S. E.,
And "straddled" the market in glee.

I waited to see the rise in U. P.,
The long wished for bulge in O. T. ;
But, 'twixt you and me, the "bears" made me flee,
And got all I dropped in U. P.

I caught a great haul at last in St. Paul,
    And played it, "according to Hoyle,"
With brokers and "bears," who brought all my
    cares,
    And robbed me once more in crude oil.

I tried wheat and lard ; also, Grant & Ward,
    With contracts procured on the sly ;
In "short" and "long" grain they got me again,
    And profits were "all in my eye."

I'll say to the "boys," "don't court 'future' joys,
    And wish to be happy in life ;
So keep out to-day, let stocks run away,
    And give your 'collat.' to your wife."

Thus take my advice without any price,
    'Twill serve you in famine or fame ;
For soon you will find, the fool's left behind
    That tackles another man's game !

REST.

(IN MEMORY OF GENERAL O. E. BABCOCK, U.S.A.)

REST, soldier, rest beneath the sod—
Mortality has gone to God:
Thy battles o'er, all trials past—
Peace to your ashes, rest at last.

The coming years will always tell
You did your duty nobly—well—
And faced the storm when others fled ;
But now, alas, dear friend, you're dead.

Sweet be the flowers above your tomb,
Let honor in eternal bloom
Entwine the ivy o'er thy dust—
An evergreen of love and trust.

The Capital you made so bright,
Shall ever think you good and right ;
While coming years shall sound thy praise,
And memory to thy image raise

A marble shaft, to tell all time
That Genius reigns in every clime ;
And man, at last, is always just,
Because he loves and lives to trust.

While ocean billows toss and roar
Against the great Atlantic shore,
Your memory in our hearts shall be
Pure as the foam upon the sea.

Rest, soldier, rest ; brave heart, be still ;
You rest in peace on yon Oak Hill,
A brother to the silent clod—
Rest, soldier, rest in peace with God !

THE EXILE.

IN other lands beyond the sea,
  My thoughts will often turn to thee ;
And gazing o'er the billows' crest
My heart shall travel to the West,
Where lies a home, the sweetest, best.

Fair land of pine and oak and ash,
Where sparkling streams forever dash,
Mid mountain crags so grand and old
Rock-ribbed with iron, silver, gold,
And fertile fields of generous mould.

The friends I knew in childhood years
Are seen with love through smiles and tears
And as my bounding bark departs—
One look, one sigh, to tender hearts—
How memory from my bosom starts !

How oft my eyes will turn in vain
To see my native land again,
And as the sail departs from view,
I'll peer across the ocean blue
To catch one glimpse of love and you.

But I am destined still to roam,
Without a country or a home,
A lonely exile bent with care,
A barren waste, both bleak and bare—
No friend to cheer me anywhere.

A FRIEND.

A FRIEND is one who knows your fault,
And knowing dares to chide you ;
Who blisters wrong with Attic salt,
And still sticks close beside you.

A friend is one who lifts you up
When sin and sorrow hover,
Then casts aside the bitter cup
And takes you under cover.

A friend is one whose words are true,
Whose purse in trial or trouble
Is ever open unto you ;
Whose heart cannot play double.

A friend is one who bends alone
Above your nameless tomb,
And keeps your memory all her own
As flowers in full bloom.

A CONUNDRUM.

WHO keeps the ocean in motion?
    I asked of the passing breeze;
It only gave back for answer,
    The sigh of the sounding seas.

And who keeps the stars still shining,
    Far up in the boundless blue;
And ocean and earth reclining
    Under the sun and the dew?

And who keeps the world still going
    Through cycles of plodding years,
Where death is reaping our sowing,
    And joy is mingled with tears?
                        I give it up.

DO NOT MOURN.

OH ! do not mourn when I am dead,
　　Compounded with the dull, cold clay
I would not have thee bow thy head
　　Or weep for me one single day.

I love too much your noble truth,
　　To cause one sigh of me when dead ;
And looking on your blooming youth,
　　Can wish no tears when life has fled.

Forget me when I've passed away—
　　Go love another for my sake,
And let your life be bright as day,
　　And pure and good as truth can make.

Oh ! do not wear that cold, black veil,
　　To blazon grief at fashion's beck ;
Nor let one throbbing, pensive wail,
　　Bemoan me when a buried wreck.

I WALK ALONE.

I WALK alone where morning beams are shin-
    ing,
  And winds are blowing o'er the stormy sea ;
I look aloft and see a silver lining
  That thrills my soul with thoughts of Deity.

I walk alone where evening shadows lower,
  Peering through the crimson clouds of fate ;
My heart beats out the lagging weary hour,
  Repeating to my soul—too late, too late.

I walk alone where mountain streams are leaping,
  And snow-capped summits reach unto the sky,
And still my nightly, silent watch I'm keeping,
  Gazing into worlds beyond that never die.

I walk alone the rugged road of life,
  Where human "may-flies" flutter, fly, and fall ;
I battle still with everlasting strife—
  Ambition, glory, and the grave—that's all !

4*

MY SWEET SUNNY HOME.

(DEDICATED TO GENERAL THOMAS L. ROSSER.)

TAKE me back to my sweet sunny home,
   Where the jessamine clambers so free,
Where the waters are lashed into foam
   On the sands by the murmuring sea.

There, the cotton plant blooms in the sun,
   And the red bird chirps loud in the vale,
And the darkey, when labor is done,
   Picks his banjo to tell me a tale.

I have wandered o'er billows so blue,
   Chasing pleasure in palace or cot ;
But my heart fondly turned to you—
   My old homestead I never forgot.

Broken-hearted, alone, how I sigh,
   For the wild vanished years of my youth ;
Where the mocking-bird sings let me die
   'Mid the friends that I loved for their truth.

MY OLD FLAG.

(TO THE 24TH KENTUCKY V. I., U.S.A.)

HOW you call me back and again renew
　　The marches and battles of " Sixty-two ; "
When your broad stripes fluttered so bright and
　　free
From Shiloh Church to the murmuring sea.

That Sabbath morning, I remember well,
When bold Johnston's boys with their "rebel
　　yell "
Rushed on our ranks like the stormy waves,
And swept your defenders to bloody graves.

You rose and fell in the front of the fight,
While Sherman held every foot on the right,
And fought with his men in the wildest glee
On the banks of the tearing Tennessee.

But the sun went down on your shattered staff,
And your silken scars, like a maiden's laugh,
Still fluttered defiance so loud and free
For a Nation, " Kentuck," and Old Tennessee.

Brave Buell came up, with his loyal band,
In the morning mist through that swampy land,
And rushed on the foe at the dawn of day—
With the loyal " blue " o'er the rebel "gray."

The sunset beams on that April day,
Brought gloom and defeat to the daring "gray ;"
And now, to these shreds, I cling so true,
For they waft me back to old " Sixty-two."

Stone River and Champion Hills might tell,
How you stood so fast in that smoky hell ;
And flapped in the winds over Knoxville town,
Where the gallant "gray" tried to shoot you down.

Dalton, Resaca, and New Hope, too,
Shattered the stars in your field of blue,
And Kennesaw lifting its brazen head,
Poured fire and destruction o'er loyal dead.

Around Atlanta you flutter'd a shred,
Where McPherson fell with his soldier dead—
When Hood like a " Texas blizzard " came
To grasp for his cause unexpected fame.

How often you fell, how often you rose,
Like the morning sun, over vanquished foes,
And held your way over mountain and lea
Until Sherman camped by the sounding sea.

ALL FOR THEE.

L ET me wander where I may;
    Love for thee can ne'er depart,
And within my inmost heart
You are prisoned like a ray,
Pure and true, with heavenly light
Shining o'er me day and night,
Beautiful as second sight.

And the world may still deride,
Cold and hollow as the tomb,
Or like trees without a bloom ;
Yet when sitting by your side
I can smile at every fate,
Facing scorn, envy, hate,
From cruel man, Church or State.

I defy the rabble horde,
Scorn their fleeting praise or blame ;
Each to me is just the same,
Nothing but a rusty sword
That I break across my knee,
Fling away so proud and free
When my heart is filled with thee.

WHEN I AM DEAD.

WHEN I am dead let no vain pomp display,
A surface sorrow o'er my pulseless clay,
But all, the dear old friends I loved in life
Can shed a tear, console my child and wife.

When I am dead let strangers pass me by,
Nor ask a reason for the how or why
That brought my wandering life to praise or
shame,
Or marked me for the fading flowers of fame.

When I am dead, the vile assassin tongue
Will try and banish all the lies it flung,
And make amends for all its cruel wrong
In fulsome praise and eulogistic song.

When I am dead, some sage for self-renown
May urn my ashes in his native town,
And give, when I am cold, and lost, and dead,
A marble slab, where once I needed bread.

When I am dead, what matters to the crowd?
The world will rattle on as long and loud,
And each one in the game of life will plod
The field to glory, and the way to God.

OAK HILL.

(GEORGETOWN, D. C.)

GRAND home of the dead, I mourn as I tread,
    Near the forms that crumble below ;
How sad and how still the graves at Oak Hill,
    In the quiet evening glow.

Here's an old, old stone, moss-grown and alone,
    Where time has left not a trace
Of the name it bore in the days of yore,
    When the body ceased its race.

Vain, vain is the thought, no man ever bought
    Exemption, from final decay ;
To live, and to rot, and then be forgot—
    The fate of the quick of to-day.

FAR DOWN THE LANE.

FAR down the lane I see again
   A school-girl and a boy ;
They skip along with laugh and song
   In all their youthful joy.

The flowers bloom with sweet perfume,
   And everything is gay ;
This happy pair, devoid of care,
   Clasp hands in sunny May.

The years pass on, their youth has gone,
   Yet still they cling together ;
While strands of gray, from day to day,
   Proclaim the wintry weather.

But in their eyes, those love-lit skies,
   Come back o'er hill and plain,
And shine as blue, on hearts as true
   As those far down the lane.

Thus, one by one, when we are gone,
   In sunshine and in rain,
The girls and boys will have their joys,
   In skipping down the lane.

A FIRESIDE MEMORY.

SHE'S gone, yet memory unconfined
    Has reared a temple in my heart,
Where all her virtues are enshrined,
    That never from my soul depart.

Her voice, like music low and sweet,
    Could soothe me in the deepest woe—
How willing were her flying feet
    To serve me in the long ago.

Her face, like yonder bank of flowers,
    Shone brightly o'er me, near and far—
Lit up my life in lonely hours—
    My truest friend, my polar star.

No more those footsteps run to greet
    My lagging moments, night or day;
We never more on earth shall meet—
    My joys with her have passed away.

Her image hangs on yonder wall
    Still speaking of the olden time,
When she to me was all in all
    And love was in its early prime.

Now bending o'er the smouldering fire,
  I see the shadows come and go,
While one by one the sparks expire,
  And flake by flake comes down the snow.

But through the gloom I always see
  A ray of that dear vanished light,
And memory fondly brings to me
  Her image ever pure and bright.

AMONG THE HILLS.

AMONG the hills where summer rills,
   Come leaping o'er the grasses,
I hear the glee from tree to tree,
   And see the lads and lasses.

The laughing noise of girls and boys,
   Awaken youthful dreaming
Of long ago, with joy and woe,
   And many bright eyes beaming.

But now to-day my hair is gray,
   The wrinkles o'er me creeping ;
My youth is past, and here at last
   I'm left to silent weeping.

But memory clings and love still sings
   Among the hills of childhood,
The tunes I knew when friends were true,
   And pleasure ruled the wildwood.

Laugh on sweet youth, with love and truth
   Be happy without measure,
While song and rhyme can kill old Time
   And youth remains a treasure.

RETROSPECTION.

(DEDICATED TO MISS M. L——M, V.)

I SEE before
　　A cottage door
The form I loved in days of yore.
　　Her words to me
　　Were light and free
As airs upon some summer sea.

　　The garden bloom
　　With sweet perfume
Came stealing round each nook and room ;
　　The birds of spring
　　Would soar and sing,
While bees were buzzing on the wing.

　　A cooing dove,
　　She sang of love
And led me to a world above,
　　Where, pure and bright,
　　Both day and night
We'd live amid celestial light.

Her eyes of blue—
A sapphire hue,
Shone o'er me fondly, bright and true ;
And in that face
I still can trace
The beauty of her modest grace.

And she was fair
With dark-brown hair—
Her voice rang out upon the air
Like vesper bells
In convent cells,
When love its holy music tells.

She said, "some day"
We'll sail away
O'er bounding billows fringed with spray ;
And for awhile
We'll bask and smile
Within some sweet enchanted isle.

Our magic boat
We cast afloat
From summer sands and castle moat,
And swept along,
With love and song,
Till ocean wind grew loud and strong.

Far, far away
The island lay—
A tropic isle within a bay,
Where storms sleep
Within the deep
And love its holy vigils keep.

The clouds grew dark
Around my bark,
The petrel sang, and not the lark—
A thunder roll
From pole to pole
Came sounding o'er my sinking soul.

I rose and fell,
Yet could not tell
That sea-nymphs sang her funeral knell;
The rocky shore
Was right before,
And dashed my hopes forevermore.

Down in the wave
Of ocean's cave,
She sleeps within a coral grave
And dreams of me
Beneath the sea
While winds are blowing o'er the lea.

Ah ! thus we find,
When love is kind,
Some cruel fate will strike us blind,
And steal away
The sunny ray
That shines upon our life to-day.

Though hope be gone,
I'll still hope on,
And ever think of thee, dear one,
Until " some day "
I'll sail away
To greet you in a brighter bay.

BOAST NOT.

" **B**OAST not thyself of to-morrow,"
   All of this life is to-day ;
Joy is still mingled with sorrow—
Loved ones are passing away.

" Boast not thyself of to-morrow,"
   Its flowers and its fortune will fade ;
Why should we stop, then, to borrow
   The trouble that each heart has made.

" Boast not thyself of to-morrow,"
   This life is a span and a breath ;
How cold, how damp, and how narrow—
   The portals that point us to death.

Boast not, take heed lest thou fall,
   Vain pride is the runner of fate,
The grave grass shall grow o'er us all—
   The worst or the best of the state.

Boast not of this flitting hour—
   It speeds like a bird in its flight—
Frail as the dew on a flower,
   Bleak as the darkness of night.

Boast not when pleasure surrounds thee,
　Where mirth lights the garish saloon ;
All of its flash will confound thee,
　And leave thee in sorrow too soon.

Boast not at all, but be humble ;
　Do good for the sake of the good,
All that are human must stumble,
　And each heart has done as it could.

SHADOWS ON THE WALL.

THE maple grows in beauty outside my classic
    hall,
Its branches kiss my windows, and shadows climb
    the wall ;
They flit in fairy dances where Zephyr plays his
    tune,
And birds of brightest plumage sing all the airs
    of June.

The sunlight and the shadows that intermingle
    here
Bring pictures of the faces, ever pure and very
    dear,
That thrilled my heart in childhood when life
    was fresh and true,
And every changing shadow brought pleasure to
    my view.

The leaves upon the maple are dancing light and
    free,
They limn their loving features in the halls of
    memory ;

And as they murmur gayly to entrance my rural
    scene,
They bring back cheering voices with a chorus in
    between.

The shadows of the comrades I loved in long ago
Are flitting in my vision ; their faces well I know ;
And from the roar of battle I hear their voices
    rise,
To mingle with our triumph and echo in the
    skies.

And in the hall of memory, engraven fond and
    dear,
The shadow of my True Love appears from year
    to year ;
The maple never murmurs but I hear her magic
    rune—
A rose of radiant beauty that I lost in jealous
    June !

THE SUTLER.

"I will a Sutler be that profits may accrue."—SHAKSPEARE.

(DEDICATED TO THE GRAND ARMY OF THE REPUBLIC.)

I SING the song of the sutler,
   Who fought in the battle of life,
The song of the prize-package "artist,"
   Who never got into the strife ;
Not the jubilant song of the soldier
   Who never forgot to lay claim,
To the greenbacks that stuck in the "Jack Pot"
   At the end of a winter-night game.
But the song of the beautiful sutler,
   Who travelled in sunshine and rain,
For the sake of the almighty dollar
   And whatever else he could gain ;
And his youth bore no flower on its branches,
   But his age was a bright, sunny day ;
For the prize that he gloriously grasped at,
   Was the cash that he carried away.
And the work that he did for the army
   In the rear of the soldiers, was seen,
Where he set up his crackers and herrings,
   And the smell of the festive sardine,

That he sold to the " boys " on a credit,
   Or the clamp of a paymaster's lease ;
And six boxes he gave for five dollars,
   While the rest brought a dollar a piece.
While the world at large sheds a tear
   To the hero that may be bereft,
I drink to the Grand Army Sutler
   Who never was known to get left !
Who rushed to the front, when the camp-fires
   Lit up all the hills, without fear ;
But at the first crack of the rifle
   He galloped away to the rear,
With his pipes, his tobacco, and whiskey,
   And his barrels of sour lager beer ;
And he never let up on his running
   Till the Long Bridge appeared to his view,
Where he opened up shop in his wagon,
   And roped-in the gay " boys in blue."
How he held to his faith unseduced,
   With the glint of the cash in his eye ;
And for this great cause how he suffered !
   For the cash, not the country, he'd die !
Then rear to the sutler a temple,
   Of granite and brass that will stay,
Where the spirit of Shylock shall hover,
   And beam on the " blue " and the " gray,"

Who once paid a tribute to genius,
  With a gall that no mortal could rule,
And a smile like a lightning-rod pedlar,
  And a cheek like the Grand Army Mule!

THE TRAMP.

(A SATIRICAL SONG, NOT POETRY.)

THE tramp gets up in the morning, boys,
  To take the early air ;
He goes to the brook and washes himself,
  Then looks around the square.
He finds himself a shady nook,
  And there he does lie down,
And then he gets up and scratches himself,
  And walks around the town.

CHORUS.

Sleeping in a box-car,
  Tral, lal, lal, lal, lal, la ;
Chewing stubs with little boys,
  Tral, lal, lal, lal, lal, la.
We are three chums, three jolly old "bums,"
  We live like royal Turks ;
We have good look in getting our "chuck,"
  Bad luck to the man that works.

I heard a word the other day
   I never heard before :
A man he asked me how I'd like
   To go a digging ore.
I asked him what the salary was ;
   " A dollar and a half a ton."
Says I, " Old man," go soak your head ;
   I'd darn sight rather bum."

—Chorus.

The tramp goes up to the lady's door,
   And he hits the door a bang ;
He asks the lady of the house
   For " chuck " to feed the gang.
The lady says she has no bread ;
   She's just a-going to bake.
The ugly old tramp he turns around,
   Says, " I'll take pie or cake."

—Chorus.

WASHINGTON MONUMENT.

REAR to the sky a monument so grand
        That it shall shine across this mighty land,
And while the planets in their cycles run
'Twill tell the story of great Washington.
The Old Dominion claims his noble birth,
This Great Republic is his home and hearth,
While every stream shall mingle with his name
And glorious battle-fields prolong his fame.
Lexington and Concord and Bunker Hill—
Proud names that make the patriotic thrill,
Who fight for Liberty in any clime,
And die as martyrs down the change of time.
Old Monmouth, and Trenton and Brandywine,
Are links of freedom that shall ever shine
In chains that bind the love we all transfix
Around the heroes of old " seventy-six."
Saratoga, through Arnold and through Gates,
Was snatched from England by the thirteen States,
And Yorktown capped the climax of our cause,
By stamping out the cruel British laws.
Long may we live to hear the tale and tell
How Montgomery and his heroes fought and fell

Upon the frowning heights of old Quebec,
A sacrifice in freedom's glorious wreck !
Old Ethan Allen, and brave Warren, too,
Bring back the memory of the bold and true,
With Stark and Wayne and Marquis Lafayette,
And Green and Steuben that we can't forget ;
Yet while we praise the man who lost or won,
The first in all our hearts is Washington ;
Like some grand mountain shining from afar,
Or like the radiance of the morning star,
Spreading its silver light throughout the gloom
That gilds the glory of his classic tomb.
Mount Vernon keeps his loved and sacred
      dust—
An urn of grief that holds a nation's trust,
Where pilgrims bend along the waning years
To gaze upon his grave through pearly tears.
This monument in coming years shall stand
A Mecca for the brave of every land,
And while Potomac waters flash and flow
The fame of Washington shall gain and grow
Adown the ages through the aisles of time,
A patriot forever in his prime !
He broke the chains the tyrànt had entwined
Around the body and the fruitful mind,
And though starvation reigned at Valley Forge
He crushed at last the cohorts of King George,

And gave to every man the right to be
An equal in a land where all are free!
The shafts that dot the Tiber and the Nile,
Great pyramids of stone, a pile on pile,
Still glorify some queen or royal king,
Yet to our sighing hearts can only bring
The march of slaves and captives in their train—
A triumph o'er the wounded and the slain.
No slave pollutes our fatherland to-day:
Around this marble pile the good can say,
And swear in truth and faith at Freedom's shrine,
That we are brothers of one honest line.
From Boston town to Richmond on the James
Our record shines with noble, glorious names
Who fought and fell for liberty and right—
A galaxy of heroes brave and bright.
Let all the nations of the times and types
Respect our flashing flag of stars and stripes,
And come across the rolling ocean foam,
To make this blessed spot their hope and home,
While fair Columbia with her outstretched
        hands
Invites the good and true of foreign lands,
To help her build a nation free and great—
Equality the bed-rock of the State.
Age after age will sweep its course away,
The work of man will crumble and decay;

Yet on the tide of Time from sun to sun
Shall shine the glory of our Washington ;
And all the stars that in their orbits roll
Around the rushing world from pole to pole
Shall keep his name and fame as true and bright
As yonder sparkling jewels of the night.

CONEY ISLAND.

ON the beach at Coney Island
  We courted long ago,
And we pledged our love with kisses
Where waters swiftly flow.

And you told me, when the moonlight
  Lent its rays to thoughts sublime,
That your love was everlasting
  And would stand the test of time.

But you're married to another,
  And I see you on the beach,
Kissing babies as you kissed me—
  You and they are out of reach.

Yet the secret of our loving
  No one else shall ever know,
For I love you just as fondly
  As I loved in long ago.

But remember, darling Jennie,
  Though you left me in the strife,
I have a dozen babies
  And a charming little wife.

The moonlight and the sunlight,
  And the sands upon the sea,
Shine as brightly as they shone, love,
  When they shone for you and me.

Thus forever and forever
  Shall the roaring ocean screech,
And the heart of man and woman
  Will be flirting on the beach!

THE LOST ATLANTIS.

(DEDICATED TO IGNATIUS DONNELLY.)

THE night of ages is passing away,
    Yet the dawn of Atlantis shines afar,
Where the mind of man like a perfect day
    Beams out on the earth like a morning star.

There is nothing new, there is nothing old,
    In this beautiful world so fresh and free ;
The mountains are filled with silver and gold
    As they came from the hand of Destiny.

The hills and the vales will blossom in spring,
    The ocean will roar with a sullen cry ;
Old Time in his flight, with a restless wing,
    Shall whir o'er the dead without pity or sigh.

So the sun will rise and the sun will set,
    And stars will bejewel the upper blue,
And the earthquake shock like a gaping net
    Will swallow together the false and true.

I hear a voice o'er the rolling deep,
    And catch a glimpse of that far-off shore,
Where men and women will never weep,
    In the new Atlantis, forevermore.

LET'S DRINK TO-NIGHT.

LET'S drink to-night while stars are bright,
    And banish every sorrow ;
And hope to see, for you and me
    A glorious to-morrow.

Fill up the bowl and thrill the soul
    With wine of Love and Beauty ;
Whate'er you do, be always true,
    And bravely do your duty.

Laugh with the gay from day to day,
    Grieve not for vanished pleasure,
The present time we'll tune to rhyme
    And grasp it as a treasure.

CHORUS.

Cheer up, cheer up ! let's fill the cup,
    And drink to beaming eyes,
That on us shine through rosy wine,
    Like stars in yonder skies.

WHERE IS GOD TO-DAY?

(This question was asked by the five-year-old child of General
Thomas L. Rosser, Virginia.)

A BLUE-EYED boy, while sporting at his play,
    Asked this question, Pa, where is God to-
    day?
The man of years and thought could not reply,
    And only answered by the saddest sigh.

The greatest sages of the olden time
    Have asked this question of the earth and sky;
But never yet, in any land or clime,
    Has man been satisfied with the reply.

We build great temples to the God we make,
    And worship something till we're old and gray;
But from the aching heart we cannot take
    The simple question—Where is God to-day?

Perhaps the little child might tell us now,
    Where God in all his power reigns on high,
Where wreaths immortal crown the boyish brow,
    And worlds unnumbered shine beyond the sky.

VANITY.

SWEET thoughts that we cannot repeat,
  And songs that we never can sing
Arise in the brain but to meet
  And speed like a bird on the wing.

A light or a flash on the wave,
  Is the life that we live to-day—
A memory gone to the grave,
  Or the laugh of a child at play.

A glance at this world of beauty,
  A bubble that floats on the sea ;
To hope and to die for duty,
  And sink to eternity.

WHAT'S THE ODDS?

WHAT'S the odds if you're wealthy or poor?
    The day shall surely arrive
When you're carried out through open door,
    To go on your last, long ride.

What's the odds if weak or brave?
    The longest of days must end—
Hide your name in the voiceless grave,
    Without a farthing or friend.

What's the odds whether earthly power
    Shall attend your destined way?
It dies in the course of an hour,
    Like the rose of yesterday.

What's the odds if on land or sea,
    You die in want and alone,
With none to hold your trembling hand
    Or list to your parting groan?

What's the odds, so your soul is pure?
    God seeth the sparrow fall—
His love is always near and sure—
    Enough to shelter us all.

THE SHAMROCK.

THERE'S a green little plant that grows over
the sea,
That I love, although far, far away,
And its petals are always the dearest to me,
For they bloom in my heart night and day.

The rose and the lily are fine to behold,
With the perfume distilled from their cells,
But more precious to me than diamonds or gold
Is the tale that the green shamrock tells.

It tells of a faith that has never been crushed,
And a people you cannot subdue,
Of echoes of freedom that never are hushed—
Like the roar of the ocean we view.

It whispers a song of sweet dreams that are fled,
Of bright hopes that have vanished away—
Of heroes of freedom who fought and who bled,
Of bards with their musical lay.

Though the harp of the bard may be broken,
And the voice of the singer be still,
The green shamrock is ever our token—
For it blooms over valley and hill.

Where the thrush and the blackbird and linnet
   Sing their notes to the rivers that run,
And the lark can be seen every minute,
   As he circles around to the sun.

LET ME REST.

L ET me rest where sunlight lingers,
  'Neath the waving willow shade,
Where the morn with dewy fingers
  Sprinkles diamonds o'er the glade.

Where the little birds are singing
  O'er the flowers above my tomb,
And the matin bells are ringing
  Mortals to celestial bloom !

VICTOR HUGO.

STOUT heart, good man, no pomp or state
    Can gild thy pure renown—
Thy life was moulded pure and great—
    Le-Grande, in field or town.

Hater of shams, lover of right—
    A patriot sublime—
A man who ruled by love, not might,
    And wrote for all of time.

Thy memory like a sweet perfume
    Shall shine along the ages,
Be fadeless as immortal bloom,
    Or like thy golden pages,

Where love and truth are entertwined ;
    Nobility its plan—
Great royalty of heart and mind!
    You lived for God and man.

MEDORA.

(BRIDE OF A. C. D.)

L ET joy run its measure and wedding-bells
tune,
Where manhood and beauty have met at high
noon ;
To Medora and pleasure the wine-cup we'll drain,
To her health and her beauty we'll drink once
again.

Now, fresh as the morning and pure as the light,
    May her pathway be strewn with roses so bright,
And faith and fond love be her portion and pride—
    While Adelbert, the hero, clings close to his
    bride.

May the wreath of her bridal-night never more
    . fade,
    Be as dear as the home where in childhood she
    played ;   .
And her friends be as true as the stars in the sky,
    And as constant as love and "the All-seeing
    Eye."

As the years pass away and her dear friends de-
　　part,
　Let her cherish the loved ones so close to her
　　heart ;
And through every shadow in sorrow and gloom,
　Love and truth shall abide o'er the tears of the
　　tomb.

JUST SO.

OUR vices are printed in "caps,"
   Our virtues in small "nonpareil;"
And all of our daily mishaps
   The neighbors are ready to tell.

If you stumble, beware of the crowd—
   It's callous, and heartless, and cold;
'Twill praise you to-day long and loud,
   To-morrow, 'twill damn brave and bold!

MY NATIVE LAND.

FAREWELL to the land of my birth and my
childhood,
Where the shamrock and hawthorn bloom in
the vale,
And the linnet and thrush sing sweet in the wildwood ;
Where perfume of roses is borne on the gale.

Farewell to the hills and the streams where I
wandered,
To my dear mountain cot at the edge of the glen,
Where often, in spring-time, I played and I pondered,
But ne'er shall I witness those loved scenes
again.

Farewell to the church and the school-house of
learning,
To the lads and the lasses that frolicked in glee ;
My heart is near breaking while footsteps are
turning
To a land full of freedom far over the sea.

Farewell to the grave of my father and mother;
  The daisy and violet bloom o'er their head;
The turf is still fresh on the breast of another—
  The dearest and sweetest of those with the dead.

Farewell, we must part, and the links of love
      sever,
  Yet tears of remembrance for thee shall renew
The friendship I'll cherish forever and ever
  Wherever I wander, dear Erin, for you!

KISSING O'ER THE BARS.

(A SONG.   DEDICATED TO "GYPSIE KROH.")

I HAD a little sweetheart, her name was Jennie
        Lee,
We met down by the brooklet, and by the waters
        free,
We clasped and kissed each other, beneath the
        rising stars—
Our hearts kept tune together while kissing o'er
        the bars.

Although the years have left me and I am old and
        gray,
I can't forget the gloaming that long since passed
        away ;
Yet while my life is wasting and marked by many
        scars,
I'm standing by the brooklet and kissing o'er the
        bars !

Often in the evening when I gaze across the sea,
My soul is filled with rapture for home and Jennie
        Lee,

And though a lonely exile exposed to jolts and jars,
I'm kissing, fondly kissing, my sweet Jennie o'er
the bars!

She left me in the morning when life was young
and true ;
Her spirit shines upon me from yonder bounding
blue,
And though the world rebukes me with many
winds and wars,
My heart and soul feel rapture, while kissing o'er
the bars!

.

THE MYSTERY.

I LOOK upon Nature and gaze on the sky,
   To solve its deep problem I wearily try :
The ocean that roars on the wild rocky shore
Chants a mass to my soul—I heard once before,
In the millions of years I lived in the past—
As fleet as the lightning, and fresh as the blast
That blows in the spring over blossoming flowers
When the Day God of life counts the pulse of the
      hours.
Old Time, with the whir of an eagle proceeds,
And rushes along like the battle-scarred steeds
That trample together the high and the low, .
And dash to atoms the friend and the foe.
But Time is immortal, and so is the soul,—
This life but a threshold to God as our goal,
Where love is unending and Death does not wait
To spurn a poor mortal who knocks at the gate,
That leads to the Uplands, away from this sod,
Where virtue is virtue and Glory is God.
The body will change but the soul cannot die,
To fathom the Godhead 'tis useless to try.

We come and we go like the coquetting breeze ;
We rise and we fall like the tide of the seas,
That break on the shore with its murmuring spray,
To sparkle a moment, then vanish away.

OBLIVION.

A WRECK on the beach, a cry on the shore,
    Where the storm-king roars his call—
A break of the wave and forever more
    Oblivion covers us all.

It covers the good, it covers the bad,
    It covers the young and the old ;
It buries the gay, the silent and sad—
    The false and the true and the bold.

It reigns over land, it reigns over sea,
    A murky, mysterious cloud—
No silvery lining for you or for me,
    But funeral palls for the crowd,

That march away to a realm of night,
    Where silence and darkness prevail,
Where Time may forever cease in his flight
    To ride on the wings of the gale.

Oblivion! region of silence and rest,
    Where memory ceases to be—
Out in the wilds of a sunless west,
    On the sands of a shoreless sea !

THE THISTLE.

(DEDICATED TO THOMAS SOMERVILLE.)

LET England boast of ivy green,
　　Of beef and gold and gristle ;
But still my soul shall always lean
　　To Scotland and its thistle.

Old Ireland may its shamrock praise,
　　Romantic airs still whistle ;
Yet give me back my childhood days—
　　Dear Scotland and its thistle.

Gay France may boast the lily white,
　　Its slopes with vines may bristle,
Yet all its joys both day and night
　　Can't vie with Scotland's thistle.

Columbia, my adopted land,
　　Sweet liberty, thy story ;
To thee I freely give my hand,
　　My heart for Scotland's glory.

The land of Wallace, Bruce, and Burns,
　　Refreshed by Highland misle,
To thee my throbbing heart still turns,
　　My Scotland and its thistle.

'Tis there the bonny Doon and Ayr
    Reflect the evening shadow,
With thistles growing everywhere
    'Mid mountain, marsh, and meadow.

THE HEAD AND THE HEART.

THE Head and the Heart had a quarrel one
day,
As to which was at fault for the other;
The Head with great arrogance always would say
That the Heart was a wild, reckless brother.

And the Heart would not listen to reason ;
Yet it worked brave and strong all the hours,
While the Head tossed about in high treason
As it talked on the nature of flowers.

And the Heart with its warm pulsation
Made many a grievous mistake,
But 'twas always on side of salvation
For the poor fallen woman, or Rake.

The Head was a dastard old miser,
Who doubted the whole of mankind,
And told the poor Heart to be wiser
And leave its pulsations for mind.

But the brave Heart replied in its glory,
  I would rather be fooled now and then,
Than list to your cold, cynic story
  And doubt all my good fellow-men.

The Head was a ready-cash banker,
  While the Heart was a Prodigal Son,
And though his fair form grew lanker,
  His truth and his love weighed a ton.

If you met him in anguish or sorrow,
  In the walks of old Vanity Fair,
A shilling or pound you could borrow,
  And his smile could be found everywhere.

But the selfish old Head turned coldly,
  And vaunted its pelf and its pride,
As he passed by his fellows so boldly,
  Where they starved, and they bled, and they died.

But old age struck this top-heavy creature,
  And left him alone with his tears ;
Not a friend to gaze on his feature
  As he sank to his grave without tears.

Yet the noble old Heart with its failing,
  Had the prayers of the poor and the just,
And a funeral train all bewailing,
  When it passed to the sad, silent dust.

A THOUGHT.

WHEN the slanting beams of evening,
  Fall on my velvet lawn ;
When the heart is full of grieving,
  At early, rosy dawn—
Then I think of one, departed,
  Who faded, fond and true,
And left me broken-hearted,
  With vacancy in view !

PERHAPS.

PERHAPS when I have passed to dust,
    And sleep beneath the willow,
Some faithful heart with love and trust
    May decorate my pillow

With sweetest flowers of early spring ;
    A wreath of love's entwining,
Near where the blue birds swing and sing
    And morning beams are shining.

Perhaps when I have passed away,
    My words in life may live and last,
And soar above my crumbling clay
    Where stands a monumental shaft

That tells the passer-by my fame ;
    A marble tribute o'er my head,
A stone to signalize my name,
    By those who now refuse me bread!

Perhaps the world will then declare
    The good I always cherished,
And give me glory everywhere,
    When life has rudely perished.

But now to-day when seared and gray,
  With form that's bent and broken,
A lonely lay I pipe and play
For loving words unspoken.

What mockery this goal of care!
  This vain and fleeting station,
A shining show, a garish glare,
  A grand and mighty nation—

That rushes o'er the brink of fate,
  In hoards of pain or pleasure,
And finds at last, when it's too late,
  That life has little treasure!

CONSTANCY.

K. J.

I LOVE you so, I love you so,
  Yet this the world shall never know ;
Old Fate has forced our paths apart
And chilled the beating of my heart.

I dare not hope that here below
Our dreams shall full fruition know,
The love that came as Heaven's breath
Shall light me to the gates of death.

I dare not voice the thoughts that rise
Responsive to your soul-lit eyes,
Or break the spell which silence weaves
Around a loving heart that grieves.

THE VOICE OF THE CLOCK.

(DEDICATED TO DERWIN DE FOREST.)

TICK, tick, the moments fly,
  Tick, tick, we live and die.
Tick, tick, goes the hour,
Tick, tick, fades the flower.

Tick, tick, heart beats go,
Tick, tick, weal or woe.
Tick, tick, soon are fled,
Tick, tick, lost and dead.

Tick, tick, days and years,
Tick, tick, smiles and tears.
Tick, tick, wind and wave,
Tick, tick, grief, the grave.

THE WHISPERING TREES.

OH, the whispering trees, what tales they tell
　　Of a hundred years ago,
How they sprung from the secret acorn shell,
　　Near the homestead sweet and low.

The father and mother have gone to rest,
　　But the childish glee of yore
Still sounds and sings with a rollicking jest,
　　Round palace and cottage door.

The boy and the girl, the woman and man
　　Have come and gone like a dream,
But the trees that have more than human plan,
　　Tattle their tale to the stream.

A tongue in each leaf, a voice in each limb,
　　Tells me the old, old story
That fond love and truth are always with Him,
　　Great in His power and glory.

Then whisper away in the summer time,
　　Sing the song of creation,
The orchestry chime of these ancient trees,
　　Tells the tale of a nation.

A TOAST.

HERE'S to the girl of gladness and beauty,
   Who's always alive to hope, love or duty ;
Who fills up the cup and empties the bowl
To the choice of her heart, the pride of her soul.
Who's merry and happy with love, song and
      dance,
Pleased with the pleasure of life in a trance—
Sunshine and flowers make up her romance.

Here's a toast to the lass so kind, true and free,
Who quaffs off a cup to memory and me,
And wafts o'er the billow her sighs of regret
For hours that are gone and suns that are set.
One, changeless as fate, who loves to the close
Her wandering hero, through strife and repose,
Fresh in her beauty as dew on the rose.

KISS WHILE YOU CAN.

K ISS while you can ; wait not for to-morrow ;
　　The form that you love may wither in
　　　sorrow ;
The lips that you press in passion to-day
May fade in a moment, and vanish away.

The dark raven locks that glisten to-day
Soon are supplanted by silvery gray ;
The fire in the eye and bloom on the cheek
Will vanish in air, then others we seek.

Cherish the hearts and the brave, hoary head—
True in old age as when first they wed ;
Lavish sweet love on each other to-day ;
Remember, my darling, we're passing away.

Time, in his flight, will not stop to debate ;
Richest inducements will not make him wait ;
Then while he is here, let's brighten the hours,
And sparkle and shine like dew on the flowers.

Sigh not and brood not o'er gems that are lost ;
Year after year buds are killed by the frost ;
Tears will not bring back the lips that are fled—
The kisses we gave are gone to the dead.

TWENTY YEARS.

(A MEMORY OF MOUNT STERLING, KY.)

TWENTY years are gone to-morrow
  Since these streams and hills I knew ;
Twenty years of joy and sorrow
  Brings me back, dear hills, to you.

Many friends I loved are sleeping
  On the crest of yonder hill ;
'Neath the willows gently weeping,
  Near the sound of Perry's mill.

Beaux and beauties that I cherished
  Left me in their early bloom,
Yet their memory never perished
  With the blight that blurs the tomb.

Raven locks no more are shining ;
  Lost and gone the flowers of May ;
Yet how vain is all repining
  In my crown of silver gray.

Vanished voices in the twilight
  Float above the hill and plain ;
Call me fondly to the skylight,
  Thrill my heart with love again.

MATTIEVAN.

I 'M dreaming of my darling, night and day ;
   My life with her is one sweet, perfect plan ;
Her bright eyes, like the sunshine of the May,
   Sparkle love, and whisper : " Mattievan."

Her voice comes in the midnight lone,
   And lingers at my pillow, but to scan
A heart that beats for one sweet girl—my own,
   My darling little sweetheart—Mattievan.

Just see her in the waltz, so light and free !
   A jewel on the breast of any man.
She may flirt with all the world but me—
   My own dear, little sweetheart—Mattievan.

MY LITTLE ROBINS.

THE twilight deepens in the rosy west,
    My truant robins seek their downy nest;
All day long their little feet have wandered,
And I upon their sport have fondly pondered,
And set my soul upon the years in view
When baby robins shall their love renew ;
When little darlings from the parent home
Will spread their wings in other climes to roam,
And leave me in the twilight sad and lone,
To muse upon the beauties once mine own.
Will all the birdies that I nursed and dandled
Think of mother dear who fondly handled
The little wings and tired, tiny feet
That snuggled at my breast, so pure and sweet ?
And will the winter, with its chilling snow,
Bring back no sunbeams to my clouded woe ?
Or must I look beyond the grass-grown tomb,
To see my sweet ones in celestial bloom ?

THE FIRST KISS.

IN the month of November, the day I remember,
   Now gazing o'er mountain and plain,
My heart travels back to that flowery track,
   And lives in the light of her eyes once again.

How glorious and bright were the stars of the
      night,
   With the whip-poor-will tuning his song,
When our hearts were so true, and I lov'd only
      you,
   In that multitude rushing along.

The day never comes, and the night never goes,
   But I sigh for the woodland and stream
Where we sat in the moonlight, living in love
   In that bright, sunny land, like a dream.

Many years have gone by, still I sadden and sigh
   For the musical strains of the past ;
My heart fondly turns to incense, and burns
   On the altar of love to the last.

One by one we step out to that land full of doubt,
  Where hope only leads up the way
To a realm of bliss, where an angelic kiss
  Bids us welcome to eternal day.

The lips of an angel can never impart
  A pleasure so pure and so true
As I felt in my soul and my fluttering heart,
  In the moonlight, when I first kissed you.

MASONIC BRIGHT LIGHT.

HERE'S the Templar Knights from the East
and the West,
Children, children, won't you follow me?
From the North and the South we all march
abreast,
Halle, halle, halle, hallelujah!
No more do we march as the Gray or the Blue,
* Children, children, won't you follow me?
But our plumes are white, and our hearts are true,
Halle, halle, halle, hallelujah!

CHORUS.

In the morning, in the morning, by the bright
light,
When Gabriel blows his trumpet in the morning.

As a warrior band we march to the fight,
Children, children, won't you follow me?
Our swords shall flash in the cause of right,
Halle, halle, halle, hallelujah!

The poor and the weak we are pledged to protect,
  Children, children, won't you follow me?
We are Christian men, without any sect,
  Halle, halle, halle, hallelujah!

CHORUS.

Then up with the cross, and a cheer for the crown!
  Children, children, won't you follow me?
The Crescent of the Pagan is almost down,
  Halle, halle, halle, hallelujah!
Then hurrah for the girl that we all love best!
  Children, children, won't you follow me?
From the North, the South, the East, and the
    West,
  Halle, halle, halle, hallelujah!

CHORUS.

MY WAR-HORSE, "BOB."

(IN MEMORY OF COL. CHAS. D. PENNYBACKER'S PET.)

FAREWELL, farewell, my beautiful bay !
　　Sadly I sigh for your loss to-day ;
My thoughts go back to the long ago,
Where we tramped and fought with the deadly foe.

Of all the friends that I ever knew,
None served me so kind, so brave, and true.
Ah ! how shall I tune this nameless lay
In memory of my dear old bay ?

No bugle note shall ever again
Call thee to muster on hill or plain,
Where passion and pelf cause men to bleed ;
　No more shall I ride my gallant steed.

In the days of war, when blood flowed free,
We campaigned together, you and me ;
Now, who can blame me to grieve and sob
For losing my friend, my war-horse, " Bob ? "

Brave comrades have fallen by my side ;
In the battle-ranks they fought and died ;
Yet, even these heroes, young or gray,
Were not more prized than my noble bay.

THE DAYS ARE GROWING SHORTER.

THE days are growing shorter every hour,
    And all the sweets of life are turning sour ;
The morning dawns to me without a plan,
And everything seems happy but frail man.

The friends I knew and loved in former years
Have vanished like the sunshine through my tears :
They fill my soul with thoughts of long ago,
And memory brings me only bitter woe.

Sweet beauties that I cherished in their bloom
Went quickly to the cold and silent tomb,
And friends that were the dearest unto me
Are lost beneath the moaning, weary sea.

The evening star is beaming soft and lone,
The forest trees are bending with a groan,
And in my heart there springs a nameless grief ;
The grave alone must bring its sure relief.

The midnight's hour approaches, sad and still,
Wild phantoms come and go against my will ;
Yet, through the fearful gloom methinks I see
A blissful vista to eternity.

THE ATTORNEY-AT-LAW.

A N attorney-at-law lately put up his shingle,
    And had scarcely enough of the specie to
        jingle.
He said to himself : " I shall work long and late
To find a rich will or a bankrupt estate."

So he sat in his office and puffed, day by day,
Forming rings of blue smoke that floated away,
While, with Parsons and Kent, and Blackstone and
        Chitty,
He appeared to his neighbors so wise and so witty.

At length a rich miller, by name Calvin Brown,
In search of a lawyer, came into the town,
And spying a smoker, he thought he would pin
        him,
And marched up the stairs to the office of Skin'em.

"Good morning," said Brown, to the lord of the
        laws ;
" I've come to consult for the good of my cause."
" Be seated," said Skin'em ; " I know you'll be
        gainer,
But first, I require, now, a thousand retainer."

Brown stared in surprise at this heavy demand,
And said it was more than he felt he could stand ;
But the "limb of the law" a glance at him flings,
He puffed his cigar, and went on making rings.

The miller, at last, like the fly in the fable,
Was caught in the web ; where, entirely unable
To cope with the spider that bled him so neatly,
He gave up the ghost, and passed off completely.

* * * * * *

Skin'em is now the sole administrator ;
And you may be sure that, sooner or later,
The widow and orphans of one Calvin Brown
Will be out of a home, and put on the town.

Then Skin'em will shine as a brave lady-killer
On plunder he filched from the honest old miller,
And the people will gaze on his rich turn-out,
And say to themselves : " How did this come
    about ? "

Poor dupes ! you are fooled by the gauze and the
    glitter ;
You begin with the sweet, and end with the bitter ;
And fellows like Skin'em lay ever in wait
To pounce on the bones of a crumbling estate.

Thus the law, you must know, is made for the
    rich,
And the poor, as of old, are left in the ditch ;
No matter what rights you may have to maintain,
You'll lose in the end, should you dare to "retain."

Now take my advice, and keep out of the law ;
For, once in the toils of its ravenous maw,
You are sure to be plucked, without mercy or
    grace,
And come out the last at the end of the race.

THE BOAST OF BACCHUS.

I REIGN over land, I reign over sea,
   The proudest of earth I bring to my knee
As weak as a child in the midnight of care;
The prince and the peasant I strip bleak and bare.

A taste of my blood sends a thrill to the heart,
And speeds through the soul like a poisonous dart;
While I leave it a wreck of trouble and pain
That never on earth can be perfect again.

The youth in his bloom and the man in his might
I capture by day and I conquer by night;
The maid and the matron respond to my call,
I rule like a tyrant and ride over all.

In the gilded saloon and glittering crowd
I deaden the senses and humble the proud,
And tear from the noble, the good, and the great
The love and devotion of home, church, and state.

I blast all the honor that·manhood holds dear,
I smile with delight at the sight of a tear,
And laugh in the revel and rout of a night;
My mission on earth is to blur and to blight.

I ruin the homes of the high and the low,
I blast every hope of the friend and the foe ;
The world I sear with my blistering breath,
And millions I lead to the portals of death.

In the parlor and dance-house I sparkle and roar
Like billows that break on a wild, rocky shore ;
I crush every virtue, destroy every truth
That blossoms in beauty or blushes in youth.

My power is mighty for sin and despair ;
I crouch, like a lion that waits in his lair,
To mangle the life of the pure and the brave,
And drag them in sorrow to shame and the grave.

I drown royal hearts in the dregs of the bowl ;
I sing and exult in the sigh of the soul ;
I darken the mind of the faithful and fine—
Hurrah for the Devil that reigns in the wine (?).

THE BATTLE OF SHILOH.

(DEDICATED TO THE AMERICAN SOLDIER.)

BANDS were playing, horses neighing,
  Soldiers straying, mules were braying ;
Banners flying, women crying,
Hearts were sighing, many dying ;
Onward, backward, all uproarious,
The " Gray " victorious, the " Blue " was glorious.
The field was won, the field was lost,
Like ocean billows, torn and tossed ;
And on the bloody beach of war
Waves of dead, a giant scar ;
And mangled bodies torn and pale,
Like forests in a withering gale.
Up the hill and down the vale,
Advance, retreat, but never fail ;
Fix bayonets, forward, guide right !
A shout, a yell, God ! what a sight.
At them again through smoke and fire ;
Fight and fall, but ne'er retire.
Once more to the breach, steady, strike—
Blood, broken bones, who saw the like

Never forgets through the long years
That call up our smiles and our tears.
Capture cannon, capture men,
Crash, smash, at them again.
Hark to the yell of Cleburne's men,
They rush like demons through the glen, .
Driving the " Blue " toward the river,
And many are lost forever ;
Sherman shouts "Halt ! right about, charge!"
Then down through the brush and the gorge
The " Gray " in turn are flying.
Lord ! how the soldiers are dying.
McClernand, McCook stand at bay,
While Wallace is lost on the way
To the field, where Prentiss surrenders
To the South and its brave defenders.
Cheatham, Withers, Gibson, and Bragg
Stand out like a wild, rocky crag
And beat back the bold invaders ;
At last they are crushed by the raiders.
Then Crittenden, Hurlbut, and Wood
With many brave heroes withstood—
Charge after charge, through the rain
Of bullets that whizzed o'er the plain.
Webster shouts " Park and unlimber!"
Shot and shell right through the timber—
Cannons that growl like December,

Sounds that we long shall remember,
Shriek like the roar from a burning hell,
Sending the foe to the rear pell-mell!
Danger and death so fierce and hard
To the halting troops of Beauregard!
Sunday's sun has gone at last,
Rushing rains are falling fast
On the faces cold as lead,
On the dying and the dead.
Brave Sidney Johnston led the " Gray,"
But Fate cut off his life that day,
And Beauregard could not repel
The Union fire—a blast from hell,
Where cannon thundered o'er the glen
And shattered horses, boys, and men.
Then Monday's sun arose in a gloom
And spread its clouds above this tomb,
Where Grant and Buell joined to smash
The stubborn Gray with one dread crash.
But still the Gray declined to yield,
And fought like tigers on the field—
Till wave on wave " the boys in blue "
Rolled o'er these Southern hearts so true—
While Sherman over swamp and bridge
Dashed on the gallant Breckenridge!
The day was won, the day was lost,
And twenty thousand told the cost,

Where brothers bled and brothers died—
A ruin with its crimson tide,
That flowed for you and flowed for me
On the torn banks of the Tennessee!
The sun goes down, the stars are set,
That bloody field we can't forget
While valor holds a deathless sway
And Honor crowns the " Blue " and " Gray."
It may be that the winking " stars "
Contain the men who loved the " bars "—
And that those gallant, noble types
Join hands with those who loved the stripes.
But "stars " and "bars" and " red " and " Blue "
And "stripes" and " stars " wave over you ;
One Nation fills our fame to-day—
The " red" is " Blue" and the " blue" is " Gray "!

  A thousand years of glory
   Shall immortalize our fame—
  With a tale in song and story
   To keep green the hallowed name,
  Of the victor and the vanquished
   On the land and on the sea,
  A band of noble brothers
   Led by gallant Grant and Lee.
  And the tears of beaming beauty
   Shall freshen every flower—
  In the May-time of our duty,
   Through the sunlit, fleeting hour.

Then we'll strew the rarest roses
    O'er the graves we bless to-day,
And we'll pluck the purest posies
    To enwreath the " Blue " and " Gray."
And down the circling ages,
    From the father to the son,
We'll tell on golden pages
    How the field was lost and won ;
And how a band of brothers
    Fought each other hard and true
To bind the Union arches
    O'er the " Gray " and o'er the " Blue,"
And reared a lasting temple
    So complete in every plan,
To justice, truth, and mercy
    And the liberty of man !

www.ingramcontent.com/pod-product-compliance
Lightning Source LLC
Chambersburg PA
CBHW020554270326
41927CB00006B/839